WEB' FOOT

The Web' Foot

Tricia Jones

Acknowledgement

Light of the morning

A single lamp post
stands next to a bony tree in the fog.

Previous Publications

Unweeded Garden	1991
High Water	1998
The Shield	2000
Stepping-Stone	2001
Dog-Tooth	2003
Suns Turning	2004
Dark-Lantern	2005
Sea-Cloak	2005
Broken-Water	2006
Soft-Rain	2006
Empty Bottle And Silly Half-Hour	2007
Love Doesn't Make Any Sense	2007
Melted-Icicle	2007
Overtide	2008
Dancing Waves	2009
Weather-Beam	2010
Stinging-Nettles	2011

Fire And Earth

Burning cloud
Purple streaks
A deep glow of the sun
Beginning to peep behind the roof tops
The sun rises even more like a fireball
The full round sun
Radiate and string the window
Hopping on the fresh green grass
Behind a bush
Is the unseen
The roof tops are black
With a mist over the sea
Which looks icy-cold
A bird flies on top of a twig
Over the roof tops out to sea
And against a cold window sill
The radiator burns.

Morning Sun

The sun
Is like
A hot
Water bottle
On my
Neck
My forehead
Is ablaze
I close
My eyes
The heat
Comes
Through
The window
A bird
Is gliding
Overhead
The clouds
Are fluffy
In a deep blue sky
Peace
Be still
In the wonder ness
Of nature.

Chance

He sacrificed his kidney
To a woman he never knew
He carried the donar card
In his pocket for six years
Until he no longer lived
On this earth. The siren of the police car could
Be heard for miles
Inside the police car
Was a frozen box with
Inside was a kidney
Travelling as fast as
They would go to reach
The hospital. The operation
Had already started and it
Was a tricky situation
With five minutes to go
The police car reached the
Hospital and it was hastily
Travelled to theatre in time.
The woman never knew who saved
Her life, but she would never forget the soul-searching
Gift of this Angel
God Bless.

Be Still

The sky is dark
Covering the blue
With a deep
Shade of grey
The world
Is still and pretty lights
Appear
Between
Fern trees.

Wonder

God of creator
Of Heaven and Earth
Can make a single
Snowflake fall
In a thousand
Different webs
Hand carved
By his hand.

See

Go out into the wilderness
Into the nettles.

Thorn' Set

The sun came out
A sharp hand part
Of the leaf
A hedge of hawthorn
A poisonous plant
Of the potato family,
With a prickly capsule, a haw
In all its radiance
Destroyed it
Blown by the wind.

Sleep Time

Dancing curtains
In a rhythm
To the wind
Good night and God Bless.

The Door

The stone house stood proud near
The edge of the cliff looking out to sea
To get to the back of the house
You had to cling onto hinges on the wall
Or bushes or trees
To stop you from getting
Blown off the cliff
Into the sea
I reached the back of the stone wall
It was sheltered here
There was a huge heavy wooden door
With mouldy rusty hinges
I waited
And rung a bell
It seemed like ages
Before an old grey-haired lady
Came after the creaking door opened
She had a determined
Grace about her
Asked what I was doing there
It turned out that she was once
A famous ballerina now shut away
In a beautiful cave.

Coffee Break

The sun's rays
Are on my eyelids
Shining through the pane glass
In the dining room
A radio sounds
Coming from ground level ward
The grass has shadows
And the birds sing
Amongst the music and chatter
My eyes look at the sun
And it is
Like a volcano erupting
Star-struck
Moon-beams
I shut my
Eyes and feel
Red warmth
Waiting for hot coffee.

Wonderful

Stars revolving
Around the sun
Red hot flames
Warmth, heat
Fiery laser beams
Of light
I half shut my eyes
And the windows
Echo the round shape
Of the moon
I sit in wonder
And close my eyes
And all I can feel
Is warmth, security and peace.

Sky – Blue

I know you are a star
In the sky
You have recently met Mum
And you are now together
The brightest star
In a crystal horizon.

Wild'ing

When we were children we used to climb
A mountain
Which was next to my aunt and uncle's house.
Their garden was next to the Symplon tunnel
With a winding lane, leading up the mountain
The path was alive with grass hoppers
Being in a state of nature, not tamed or cultivated
That which grows wild or without cultivation
A name for various herbivorous.
Jumping insects of the Orthoptera,
Related to locusts and crickets
That chirping by rubbing
Their wing-covers
We followed the path leading to the top of the mountain
Our uncle one day said he was going to show us something
And he took my sister and I to a room.
He opened the door and inside the walls
Were covered with glass containers containing butterflies
I didn't like it because those butterflies
Should not have been killed
They should have been allowed to live.
One day our cousins took me and my sister swimming.
I pushed the eldest cousin in the deep end
Of the swimming pool,
He swam and got out and then pushed me in,
I was only ten years old and shouted,
I could not swim
I was rescued by a passer-by
My sister and I one day we were on the path
And we saw a huge snake sliddering across the path,
We went back to the house and found a small box,
A cage and told our aunt that we were going to catch the snake
She said a definite no.

Finally we reached the top of the mountain
And there were hundreds of wild flowers
We would pick bunches and took them back
To my aunt and uncle's house.

Guardian Angel (song)

Jesus is mine
Jesus is mine
Jesus is mine
Oh, Jesus is mine
Jesus is mine
Jesus is mine
Jesus is mine
Jesus is mine
Oh, Jesus is mine
I love you Lord
I love you Lord
I love you Lord
Oh, I love you Lord
Jesus is mine, Jesus is mine
Jesus is mine, oh, Jesus is mine
You are always there, you always care
You love us Lord and we love you
Jesus is mine, Jesus is mine
Jesus is mine, oh, Jesus is mine
Jesus is mine, Jesus is mine
Oh, Jesus is mine, oh, Jesus is mine
Jesus is mine
Oh Jesus is mine
Oh Jesus is Lord.

China-Bark

Stirring a spoon, in the teapot, putting its lid back on.
Formally a tree, Camellia, sinensis, family, Theaceae
Cultivated in China, a teapot waiting on the table
To make hot,
And very dry
To roast, slightly,
To scorch.
With a plate
Of hot scones
Melted hot butter
My father used to clean the tea pot out with a hot cloth
And then put boiling water in it and then rinse it out.
He would then boil the kettle again
And he would pour the hot water into the pot with tea leaves,
Wrap a cloth around the tea pot, then get fresh cups
And pour the tea straight in,
Served on the spot and you had to drink
It straight away.
Its dried and prepared leaves, buds and shoots,
A beverage of infusing the leaves in boiling water
A thick cover for a teapot, to keep the tea hot
A medium-sized, bowl-shaped cup designed for drinking tea
Out of a kind of tea grown in China and smoke-cured
Articles of porcelain brought from China.

Dark

The rain is pouring down
In bucket loads
Forcing its way against
The windowpane
The curtains stand idle
Ignoring
The storm.

Quiet

The Sound of a cuckoo
As I drink
Early morning tea.

Empty Chair

The sun shines
Over the sea
As another
Angel
Is taken
To Heaven
The clouds are fluffy
And the sky a
Calm blue
God Bless.

Window

A crow came to see what the matter was
and flew overhead.

Branch

The sun is shining
And it is so peaceful
The grass has grown shadows
As the tall trees
Keep them in the shade
The ferns
Are waving
In a rhythm
To the breeze
The building is silent
Save for the banging of doors
To let us know
Lunch time
Is ready.

Now

Crystal sea
Under the moonlight sky
Bird's flock
Shaken from a tree
And fly free and then disappear
The sea is cold and icy
But purple, blue and pink
The deep green grass in turfs
While bird's pink worms the wind howls
Creeping around the building
The tea mug is empty as I watch from the window
And sit, the door's shut and close
I pour myself another cup of tea
The wind blows my hair
And warm my hands
On the mug.

Accept Lost Forever

I will never see his face
I did once while sitting on a wall
He passed
I don't think he saw me
Like a ghost he
Looked right through me
An innocent glance
That I would surprise me
In a moment there were rockets
And fireworks
He passed me
While I was sitting on
A stone wall
And he looked as though
He didn't recognise me
But I did.

Eternity Ring

The child
was taken away
sheer brute force
for the mother
A ring set
all round with
stones, symbolising continuity
and everlasting love
weeping and screaming
inside where nobody
would know
A precious gem
diamond shining jewel
could she
visit the child, no, too
much of a bad influence
and destruction for
the child
please bring
my babies back
I want to grow up
with them, and teach
them what I know
A passing school cry
she looks and turns
expecting to see
her two children
but it was lost in the wind.

Shiver

Fairy lights
All along
The main road
They dazzle
In the rain
Showing
The way
Home.

Music

The wind blows
And the rain pours
And a magpie says, 'Chatter, chatter, chatter.'
The window bangs
And the curtains twirl
A hurricane roars and cold air blows
Around my
Bare
Feet.

Tea

The chatter of nurses in the background
as I drink my hot cup of tea
and look down
an empty
corridor
as I sit the window blows open
and the force of the wind
pushes the door open
so I shut the window
the door remains closed
I wedge a rolled up
paper towel in the door
and the window
stays open
and amidst the hurricane
I can hear
a cuckoo
hollow sound
deeply sing.

Caller

Half
Washed
Toe nails
Covered
In
Dirt
She
Adjusts
Her
Hat to look smart
And put on her colour red
Pearls, lipstick
Finish
Into
The
Night.

Cobweb Corner

Books shut away in the corner
but the author is scared
waiting to be read
so brilliant information and devout attention
people won't like them
a pleased look to read
attention to detail
family, love, fun,
is covered in dust
in a torn out box
expression calling straight from the soul.

Inside

All I wanted
Was to join in
But my illness
Stopped me
It is always
Getting in
The way
I tried
So
Very
Hard
To
Have
A normal life
But it is
Only for
Other people.

On One's Own

One single seagull
Sitting on a chimney
Looks out to sea.

Endless

Laughter and chatter
in the dining room
evening
hot chocolate with
trifle, empty carton
chocolate in bottom of cup
time and space
In room empty
and large clean sheets
clothes ready for the morning
peace and quiet
slamming doors
shut for the night.

Tide

Walk bare feet
in the midday rain
along a sandy beach.

Day-Break

Fluttering shadows in the sun
deep cooing noises
as the
birds
wave
their wings.

Paving Stone

They live in the dark, without it they have nothing
For the sun to talk, waiting,
I swim in coal and dust and grasp my hands
like a dough making bread
A black tunnel, there is no escape
with the earth there is nothing
before or behind
tunnel,
long, dark
just stay in this.

By Star-Light

Star-light was in his eyes as he looked up without recognition
he smiled when he saw me and asked me how I was
I said, 'Alright, thank you.'
I couldn't look at him
and left him to chat with the person I was with
My fingers were tearing my nails apart
and blood came when I dug my
nails into my flesh
you feel such a fool
but it was just
one of those things.

Highlight

I was moved to a ward downstairs
Because there was a shortage of beds
Where there were elderly patients
We had a cup of tea and toast
And they were all sitting around
Watching 'Jack the Ripper'.

Morning Run

A purple and black pigeon gulped
and cooed and pecked from the grass
with his head bobbing up and down
and a large grey and white seagull
stole his bread
and flew away with it in its beak
a crow sat on a twig and squawked
with bread in its mouth
and the seagulls flapped their wings
as a man walked past with
his
dog
leading
him
down
the
grass
on the
edge of
the
winding road.

Aboriginal

He is soft,
Such as the koala, like a bear in manners
Inclining towards
A pillar of society
Keeping up with the immaculate
Overgrown daisies and buttercups
A stage
Where everything is performed
Other times like a cliff face
With bony jagged edges
Any useless plane
Of small growth
Any plant growing
Where it is not
Wanted
Amongst
Cultivated
Plants
Any wild herb,
A heavy carnivorous animal with
Long shaggy hair and hooked claws
To sell the bear skin
Before one has caught the bear
To lead about
A performing bear.
Clinging, to the underground part of a plant
The roots of a tree
You can still
Hear the cries
In the wind.

Chance

There is one
Flower left
To change the world.

Rescue

Midnight
A cruel sea
Hopeless
Wading in
Lost
The whole
World against him
Left on
The beach
To rot
Where will he go
Next
A hospital
Bed
With
Clean
Sheets on
A cuckoo
Hoots
Outside
Shadow forlorn
Figure
Face
Tears
Roll
Out underneath the stars
A nurse said,
'Are you alright.'

Crisp

The snow came
Wind-swept
Along the pathway
Dangerous ice
It is now raining
And making it
More dangerous
Turning into slush
And slippery
Black ice
The street is empty
And a cold wind blows
As I sip my tea.

Shiver

With the washing of the waves
On the shore
Spirit able guided
As the wind moans
We are
Snug inside.

See Through Glass

How dare you crow
Flying so close to my window.

Glow

The yellow sun
is echoing onto the
crystal sea
shadows line
the deep water
the moving tide
must be quite strong
as it dances
around a water mammal
which is too far away
to be recognised
but could be a sea lion
and now
there are three or four playing
amongst the waves.

Another Side Of The Dining Room

Tree you are blocking
My view of the sea.

Watching

A huge black raven and a seagull
are trotting together
on the grass
then the raven flies away
with some bread in its beak
and the seagull flies
overhead
the black raven is king of the grass
and a robin sits on a twig
and then hides in the shadow of a bush
another seagull flies overhead
with some bread also in its beak
and the sun shines
through the window
on my forehead
and I open my eyes
at this wonderful
paradise.

Por'trait Gallery

They would hang, as two different
Paintings on our wall
They never asked for nothing
They just let you sit
And if we missed a day
They would want to know
Where we had been
They were always so pleased
To see us
And made us feel at home
We would
Share our troubles
And they would share their thoughts
And we would be very protective
Towards them
And make sure they wouldn't
Come to any harm
The two portraits on the wall
'Oh Author, we are together
Again,' Harriet would say,
'I can't believe it,'
They look at us
Always.

Silence

Alone
listening to the sound of the air vent
in an empty room with
clean
sheets
a comfortable chair
a wardrobe
and they give me my own
space.
I sit here for
hours just listening to the
sounds of the birds
looking out of the window
each house in the distance
have a family
which is the most
important thing in the world
On the streets, it must be cold
how can we live in such an
unforgiveable world.

Out

The waves are cold
icy
freezing
he is enjoying himself inside
with a blazing fire
I am on the sand
with wind in my hair
salt covers my face
like a crust on bread
I try to protect myself
from this freezing wind, wrapped in
stinging nettles
was there any more
I could do
to change a situation
which was out of the moon's
Depth.

5am

Silver fairy lights glow
High on a hill
A pink and grey sky in shreds
Tweet, tweeet, tweet, tweet
Squawk, squawk, squawk
Whistle top notes
A swarm of birds fly past
In the distant orange streaks
Tweet, tweet, tweet
Screech, screech, screech, screech, screech
Eow, eow, eow, eow, eow,eow, eow
Eow, eow, eow, eow, eow,eow, eow
Sizzler, sizzle, sizzle, eow
The pink sky is fading
Into the back
And the black navy sky
Has turned purple
Puffs of cloud are slowly moving
The birds are still singing
Eow, eow, eow,
Twirp, twirp, twirp
Sizzle, sizzle, sizzle
A seagull cries
And a street lamp shines.

Arrow

Voices from the past
scribbled straight from the heart
The fitting together
in a design of small
pieces of coloured marble
glass, a piece of work of
this kind, anything of similar appearance,
or composed
by the piecing together
of different things, a leaf-mosaic,
Leaf-mosaic disease
a hybrid with
the paraental characters
side by side
and not blended
One reading hope they will get
a message to the one he loves. There
is no stopping sheer talent ready by whoever
sleeps there
or taking shelter from the wind
Did she read words
of pure love he
will never know
because her parents
disallow everything
Half a wooden heart
held by a string
worn around the neck
They will never see each
other again
but words of love
tenderly will
outlive in my mind
they whisper in the wind.

Ticket

A man got on the bus
And sat down
A mixture of
Cigarette smoke and booze, the old
Stone wall outside
When the door opened
Covered in moss
And wild flowering weeds
Peeping through
The doors open
And the bus is crowded
We go around a
Bend it was like
Being at sea again
Swaying from
Side
To
Side.

Morning Tea

The clouds are fierce, in a battle with the wind
It is dark because the sun hasn't come out yet,
The street lamps are still on,
Showing that life is asleep,
The black shaped bushes remain silent,
As twigs sprout up towards the sky,
My mouth is dry
And I am going for a hot cup of tea.

View

The trees are like pointed sticks
Only a bush with its coat
Of green stands out.

Winter

The weeping willow's
Coat of hair
Brushed early for
The summer
A seagull flies
In a thermal
Gliding
Up and away
Over the sea
I wish I
Could fly.

Nightfall

A street light shines
And a pink sky glows.

8am

The seagulls screech
In a deep blue sky
I am in the warm and it is cold outside
The fern trees are dark
Lit up by a street lamp
Next to an old wooden bench
I look again
The sky a light blue with grey fluffy clouds
A seagull does a nose dive
And the birds are chirping
It is time for their breakfast.

Small Change

He was grubby
and his hair was
overgrown
to ask for earnestly, to beseech, to pray
to fail to answer or resolve
His eyes
glistened
in the snow
and tears
fell down
his face
sitting in rugged rags, with his cap on the pavement
any small change
A complete stranger came out of nowhere
and listened to the busker
He asked him if he would like to attend an audition
with Andrew Lloyd Webber
it was a musical about Jesus
next morning prom and smart still with his long hair
went to the audition with the stranger
Andrew Lloyd Webber had been there all day listening
to hundreds of hopefuls for the part.
Then he said he was going home.
The stranger said, 'Why don't you listen to one more.'
'Oh okay,' he said.
The busker came on and sang about Jesus,
tears swelled up in his eyes as he sang,
the whole hall was transfixed
and a silence known like never before.
Andrew Lloyd Webber said immediately,
'Give him the part of Jesus.'
The busker now sings all over the world
and the stranger is now his agent.

Missing

Children playing football on the school sports field
One boy in particular was outstanding with the ball
He could play tricks kicking it
And was totally in command of the ball
Our neighbour said, 'That boy is certainly going somewhere.'
The dads would meet over a drink in the local pub
And discuss with the teachers about how their lads
Could go up the hill
Becoming outstanding football players
My brother didn't have our dad around
And this outstanding footballer never had a chance
To be picked for the teams.
He used to practice on common ground
In perfect rhythm with the ball,
But nobody supported him
And it was like a growth inside,
It bought a lump to my throat.

Whisper

The chair is no longer there
The furniture is a mixture
Of untidiness
Some of it is missing
Taken by people
We do not know
The photo albums
Are left behind
Scattered
The most important
Things in the house
I wish you were back Mum
Could it have been
Any different
With past mistakes
Blown away
By the wind
Into a silent resting place
Surrounded by members of a family
History of the past.

Angels

A family life
Is the best thing
In the world
Without it
You are nothing
But memories
Or happy times
Are in the future
With your family past and present
The most precious thing
In this world
God gave us Angels.

Song Without Music

Written lyrics
A chance in a million
The art of expression in sound
In melody and harmony
To meet musician
A social gathering with music
Blown by insecurity.

Afternoon

The sun
Red rays
A sea of orange
Disappear behind a cloud
All is cold.

Author

I used to sit transfixed.
He used to talk
For hours
About the olden days
I used to sit transfixed
And loved hearing
The local gossip about neighbours and friends
When he went to the pub years ago
With his hand cart, he would travel, walking
Pulling the cart for many miles, sometimes he would
Come home empty handed for the customers
With his chimney sweep brushes
They hadn't been in
I used to sit transfixed
He may have been a small built man
With his cap
But there was fire in his voice and his
Eyes twinkled when in
Conversation
He used to speak Welsh
When his brother came around
And it amused him when conversation
Was in the room
I used to sit transfixed
Because neither my mum-in-law or me could not
Understand a word, only when he
Said, 'Harriet, put the kettle on,'
And they would smoke and talk in deep tones
Until it was time to go
'You must come over tomorrow,' he said
And hated it if we missed a day
He is sorely missed, but his spirit lives on
Leaving a lot of happy memories behind.

Safe Haven

I feel safe
unharmed, free from danger,
secure, sound, free from risk
certain, sure, reliable
trustworthy
cautious, good, fine
To shield from danger
to strengthen
barbed wire
against
the unknown
keeping safe
and already
living a normal life
with protection
but it was only, for one night
before I was transferred back
to my ward with
sunshine.

Ovaltine And Hot Toast

Holding hands
Turning the print
Of his newspaper
Sitting, relaxing
Feet stretched
Quiet, calm, collected
I watch
The television
As he turns
Another page.

Guitar

I went to the band
And played the drums
For half an hour and at the
End I felt tired but exhilarated.

Music Room

Guitar, several people
Just dropping in and out
One man said that he couldn't read music
So I didn't feel so strange
Each playing a guitar with sound and
Melody to guide, one singing, one having
A smoke outside, improves music
Me beating drum to rhythm
A gathering of individual talent.

Shoe Lace

Klipperty clop the sound of a horse's hoof-tread
against a hard surface
down the corridor amidst the hustle and bustle
of people chattering in the background
a curved implement with a handle used
for easing the heel into the back of a shoe
I wonder if the heeled shoes are comfortable or just for show
to fit, squeeze of compress into a tight or insufficient space
the shoes are stiletto so obviously worn by a member of staff
the door is closed,
then a draught by the window opened the door
I like to have the window open
the freshness comes with pouring rain outside
and the shoes
are asleep.

Silent

He is sleeping
The paper keeps falling down as he nods off
With his glasses
Down his nose
The sports page is very interesting
Beard a glint
Of brown and silver
The central heating is switched on
Amid the freezing winds outside.

Spec'tacled Case

I look at you
looking at my
spectacles
sitting on the table
having rings around the eyes
a pair of lenses
for correcting the eye sight
mounted in frames
with side-pieces
to grip the temples
they are my eyes
for I could not
read without them.

Toasting Fork

Eating hot toast
Heating hands
Mug of tea, poured from a china teapot
On boiling
Marmalade
Tasty and refreshing
Cold outside
Mist on glasses
As the rain drizzles
On the windowpane
Warm inside
In an old comfortable arm chair
I sit back
And think of family
Get togethers
Of long ago
Crumbs of toast and marmalade
Smeared on my hands
I lick my fingers
As the wind blows
All are stars in the sky
I can sense their presence.

Shell Bark

A spittle running
from the mouth
a dancing shawl
worn to fit
scourched and cooking
Love
Warmth
Sympathy
with someonc
mending and knitting
So much torment
he couldn't speak
with
the cruel
sports of army
shell-shock
a crust
a hollow sphere
or the like sphere
a mere outside
empty case
to pester or tease
to harass
or lifeless relic
calm, peaceful
shell-star
Hiding underneath
the tree
Where is he now
I have called
but there is no one there.

Tent Caterpillar

I made a tent, when we would in the garden
have cups of tea,
we would drink it and then fold the cups away
poured from a plastic teapot.
Propped up by brooms
pegs from the line,
a strong notched peg driven into the ground to fasten a tent
there was an old blanket and we used it as a roof
inside were cushions, it helped it to stand up
an old cloth, we kept ourselves warm
we would sit and chat and we couldn't let
anyone else in our tent
hoping to see the stars
we were told to come in
for bed.

Daylight Lamp

Head
Falling on one side
Hands clasped
A slight shake
Glasses
Bent over
The time of daylight
As opposed to evening and night
Evening primrose
(Oenothera) with
Pale yellow flowers
That open in the evening
The close of the day.

Sleep

I remember the shadows
Around the room
While Mum was
On night duty
Which frightened me
The sound of a car
Would alight
Movements
Of shadows
Over the walls
My sister was fast asleep
And my two brothers
In the land of nod
They know they can rely
On me to help them
If they cannot sleep
A happy time was breakfast
We used to run down
The old wooden stairs
To golden syrup on porridge
We mixed it
And licked the spoon.

The Battle (Song)

Jesus is Lord
Jesus is Lord
Jesus is Lord
Oh Jesus is Lord
Jesus is Lord
Jesus is Lord
Jesus is Lord
Oh Jesus is Lord
We love you Jesus
Oh Jesus is Lord
We love you Jesus
Oh Jesus is Lord
We could not manage
Oh Jesus is Lord
You are always by our side
Oh Jesus is Lord
You are our Saviour
Oh Jesus is Lord
You are our Saviour
Jesus is Lord
Jesus is Lord
Jesus is Lord
Jesus is Lord
Oh Jesus is Lord
Thank you.

Beloved Ones

Peace perfect
Peace after
Having the family
Around is great
A hectic day
With a mug
Of hot Ovaltine
Relaxing
Nursery stories of warriors
And kings
Now they are
Fast asleep.

Comfortable

Sitting here
Freedom from annoyance
Just holding hands
Ease
Quiet enjoyment
Support
A magazine
Or radio
A degree of luxury
Encouragement
Sheltered
Hug close
Central heating on
Just relaxing
To manage to fall asleep
To oversleep
Wake or get up
Later than intended
Cold outside
Rain mingled with snow or hail.

Sandstones

Beautiful glazed water
A mixture of silver
And orange
A small, long-handled spade
To swim about like a duck
To dance, to walk
To add a foot to
To grasp with the foot
A place for the foot
To rest on, and stable one
Moments of time, from the use of
The grains in an hourglass
Firmness of character, grit
Black rocks
Some half-submerged
Under the sea
A representation of the sun
Often with a human face
In splendour, glory
As the central body
In a system
Flooding colours of
Pink, orange, white
Upon the calm waters.

Rescue

Midnight
a cruel sea
hopeless
wading in
lost
the whole
world against him
left on
the beach
to rot
where will he go
next
a hospital
bed
with
clean
sheets on
a cuckoo
hoots
outside
shadow
forlorn
figure
face
tears
roll
out underneath the stars
A nurse said,
'Are you alright.'

The Stone

The beach
Is lovely
Relaxing
Sitting on the wet sand
Digging with toes
Water ripples
A draft blows
Cleans your feet
Which are covered
With sand
Onto your legs
Watching the waves
To the current
Brings
A song
To my mind
In rhyme'scheme
Green and blue
Water
And swirling
With the ripples
Washing on the shore.

Pram

I am quiet but do enjoy listening
To tales of long ago
By the fireplace
With the coals lit up
And a burning orange
As flames light up the room
What they did in the olden days
How one man went on a walk with his life
A small wheeled carriage for a baby
Pushing the pram to the old coal yard
Filling the pram with coal
And covering it with a baby shawl
The village copper went up to them
And asked how the baby was
And they just scampered by
And nodded, smiling but scared
A fire was well lit that night
As they smoked their pipes
And laughed at the story.

Mem'orable

My mother-in-law when she
Was alive used to come shopping
With me. I would try
On the clothes and she would
Judge if they fitted me
Or if they looked good
We went into a cafe
And she would drink her tea
Out of a saucer but I wouldn't care
We would love to go shopping
While the menfolk
Would sit at home
Keeping in the mind
Time within which past things
Can be remembered.

Screech-Owl

One night
All our lights
Went out
It was quiet
Frightening
Everyone in the street
Had a power cut
A pace,
A movement of the leg in walking, running,
Or dancing
The distance so covered,
A footstep
In the dark
We hadn't had any food and so
Spent time with
A torch, lightening
The coal fire with rolled up newspaper and twigs
Rubbing the newspaper and blowing
Finally a spark
And the fire crackled, warming our hands
We then
Opened in the dark
A baked bean tin
Which we put the
Beans in saucepan,
Delicately held
It over the coal fire
After a few minutes it finally warmed up, the baked beans
We put them on plates in the
Dark and all of a sudden the lights came back on.

Chirp'iness

Da, da, da, da, da, da, da, da, da, da, da.
Chirp, chirp, chirp, chirp, chirp.
Sing another song or tune to change to a humbler tone
While the world
Is asleep
The ticking
Of the grandfather clock
A gallery occupied by singers
The sharp tin sound, a little bird
To give a contabile
Or lyrical effect
Singing sound, musical sand
Singing – bird a song bird
Dim light or partial darkness
The faint light after sunset
Or before sunrise
Twilight of the gods.